MY JOURNEY TO CHRIST
ENTANGLEMENT
WITH A FALSE PROPHET

Felicia Tengu

My Journey to Christ: Entanglement with a False Prophet

Copyright © 2020 by Felicia Tengu

All rights reserved. No part of this book may be reproduced or transmitted in any form or by any means without written permission of the author.

Scripture taken from the New King James Version. Copyright © 1982 by Thomas Nelson, Inc. Used by permission. All rights reserved.

Cover Design: Charles Fate (Notch Designs)

Published by:
Eleviv Publishing Group
www.elevivpublishing.com
info@elevivpublishing.com

1-800-353-0635

ISBN: 978-1-952744-01-3

Printed in the United States of America

10 9 8 7 6 5 4 3 2

Dedication

This Book is dedicated to my Heavenly Father, for loving me UNCONDITIONALLY despite all my sins and shortcomings and for never leaving me nor forsaking me even when no one was there for me. I give thanks to my Lord, Jesus Christ, for protecting and keeping me while I went through my experience with the false prophets and from all the witches and wizards who tried to kill me.

I also dedicate this book to my daughter, Zaneta Nchami, for letting me have the time to spend with God without interruptions.

Acknowledgments

I want to acknowledge my Woman of God (WOG), Evangelist Princess Belemzy, for being an inspiration to me, being so dedicated to doing the work of God, and helping me love God more. Many thanks to her for all the prayers she prayed for me and prophesying the Word from God to tell my story.

I also want to acknowledge Minister Sandra Fombi for being a friend, always encouraging, listening, and praying with me.

I acknowledge Prophet Shammar Bennett for all the prophetic words he has given to me, especially following the persecutions and abuse I got after sharing my story on Facebook. Thank you, Prophet.

I acknowledge all the followers of Jesus Loves You Unconditionally Ministries for believing in me and for continuously watching my videos, despite all odds.

I also want to acknowledge members of Princess Belemzy's Ministries for being there for me, supporting me, and watching my videos.

I can't fail to mention some of my immediate family members who have been supportive of me and my ministry in one way or the other.

Foreword

I am writing this book not because my life has been rosy; rather, I have been led by the Spirit of God to show how, through my life's mistakes and shortcomings, God was and is still with me, watching and guarding me, and waiting for me to turn to Him so He could use me for His purpose and glory.

I pray this book inspires someone to realize that God still loves them no matter what they have done in life, and He is ready to forgive them. God has his arms wide open, ready to receive all. This book highlights some of the mistakes I made in life, so readers may learn from them and spot false prophets and teachers from afar.

I strongly encourage everyone to pray about any servant of God they want to submit to after reading this book. False prophets and false teachers abound out there; they are wolves in sheep's clothing. These are men and women pretending to work for God while working for the devil. The Bible tells us that in the last days, the very elect of God might be deceived by them. I pray this book blesses you and draws you to the foot of the Cross as the prophetic word was given to me when I told my story on Facebook. God can turn your mess into your message as He did with mine. Jesus Loves You Unconditionally; never be afraid or distracted to turn to Him.

Table of Contents

Dedication

Acknowledgments

Foreword

My Childhood ...*14*

Going to School Abroad ...*22*

Graduation ...*30*

My Life at the Church ...*40*

My Entanglements with Pastor W., the False Prophet ...*52*

Exposure of the False Prophet ...*85*

False Prophets are Scammers & Voodoo Priests behind the Pulpit ...*95*

Prayer

About the Author

My Childhood

I am the second of seven children, and I have a twin brother. My childhood was an interesting one but not a bed of roses. I didn't come from a conventional family; after years of being married only to my mother, our father brought in a second wife. We just slept one night, and in the morning, there was wife number two, forever changing our family dynamics.

My father was considered a rich man in his time. He was a furniture maker, and he was very good at what he did. His furniture work even found its way to the Cameroonian Presidency. We had this beautiful white house upon a little hill, with the front made of glass.

My father had found himself a new friend, who I'm sure was sent from the pit of hell. This friend and business partner was supposed to bring new ideas to the company for the company's expansion and prosperity, but his presence only brought the exact opposite.

Father never had a relationship with God, sadly. He would sometimes drop us off at church and drive back home the instant we all got down. That is how far from God he was and the closest he ever got to church. With his new friend's help, he got entangled with voodoo priests, which hastened his downfall. It's in my father's life I saw first-hand the devil's inability to offer anything good at any time, and the validity of this scripture: The devil comes to steal, kill, and destroy.

> *The thief does not come except to steal, and to kill, and to destroy. I have come that they may have life, and that they may have it more abundantly.*
> *John 10:10 NKJV*

One day when I came back from school, I saw so many people at our beautiful white house. I was relatively young, about eight or nine, but you know children keep memories, and there were these strange-looking men doing strange-looking things in our house. These were the voodoo priests. They came right to our house, with all their demons and voodoo pots, and from that day, my father's problems got worse. He was drained and milked dry by these men. The enemy went to work and stole from my father, destroying him completely. He went into so much debt later on and had to leave the country or risk facing jail time. But this was also the enemy's plan; because the enemy finally killed him when he was out of the country.

My mom was left with seven kids to cater for. It was not easy, but God was watching over us. My mom was very strict, but her house was open to all our friends. God blessed most of her kids with wisdom; so, academic success was not a problem. Keeping up with the children's needs was not easy in any way. She was a primary school teacher with a measly pay. So, she had to supplement her income with farming. I remember sometimes we had to skip meals because of lack of food, but we were a happy bunch. My secondary and high school experiences were exciting. I was an honor-roll student with mostly A's and was always in the same class as my twin brother. We walked to school most of the time, but sometimes my friend's parents would give us a ride to and back from school. Mom couldnot afford to provide us lunch money; most times, we took food from home.

I have come a long way. Indeed, God is good. I remember times we didn't have electricity and had to use kerosene lamps for years to study. Now in the United States, I see all the amenities at my daughter's disposal, and I can tell she is blessed.

If you have not tasted hardship, you tend to take God's blessings around you for granted.

As I grew older, my siblings and I became very industrious. We made groundnut and coconut candies, packaged them in bottles, and sold them in shops. I even recall selling freshly roasted corn by the roadside. Yes, I did that. I gained street knowledge from those experiences and learned how to bulldoze and fight my way to survival. I believe the scripture that God has put everything in us that we need to prosper; we only have to dig deep into ourselves. I didn't even know God then, but He was already helping me go through life, giving me strength and hope.

> *By His divine power, God has given us everything we need for living a godly life. We have received all of this by coming to know Him, the One who called us to Himself by means of His marvelous glory and excellence.*
> *2 Peter 1:3 NLT*

Concerning church, my mom attended Presbyterian Church, and as children, we obediently followed her there. However, there was nothing like prayers or Bible reading at home. I was just a church attendee with no relationship with God whatsoever. I loved to dance and was in the ballet club at school, and sometimes we were invited to go dance at parties. We had so many friends, and many of them attended the same school as my siblings, and I did. Sometimes the ballet group used our house for ballet practice (this is not like the real ballet but a dance group called ballet) and some class parties.

School was fun. I remember once, our school's dance team was invited to perform at a party. I was doing my hair with a hot iron, trying to look pretty. This hot iron FRIED my hair; a chunk of my front hair just came off with the hot iron. I was so shocked, and my friends couldn't help but laugh at me. That part of my hair became short, but I left it as a style. As my own personal hairdresser, I had to be creative.

I loved to sleep and still do till now, I believe. I remember at night, some students went to school to read. One time, I decided to go there, but I eventually succeeded in putting my head on the desk and sleeping almost all night. Some students came and built a structure with books around my head, and I didn't even hear them. It was a deep sleep. I thank God for wisdom as I didn't have to read too much to pass my exams. My Father passed on while I was in Form Five (I was seventeen). Just a few of my relatives, my mom, and twin brother were able to lay him to rest, but life had to continue.

While I was in high school, my elder sister told me she was now a born-again Christian. I did not understand what this meant; so, I cried that day, thinking she had joined an evil cult. Besides, the people that I knew as born-again Christians in Cameroon then didn't look so good. They looked hungry and broke as if nothing was working right in their lives. Theirclothes were very unappealing, and their overall appearance a discouragement.

There was not much to my social life while I was in secondary and high school. I didn't have any relationship. I just went out on dates, and when anyone started getting serious or started asking for more than I was ready to get into, I ran away. After high school, I had to stay home for a year before going to university. I got swamped during that year, occupying myself with dating and clubbing. There was this friend who was also home and made a perfect companion for my outings. During the day, I learned how to make dresses. At night, I went clubbing with my friend. It didn't matter if we had dates or not; we still went dancing. We frequented Black and White, a club in my hometown, so much; finally, the guys who kept the doors knew us, and we didn't have to pay any more when getting into the club. While clubbing, I applied to some schools in Nigeria and got admission in one of the schools. During this time, most of my classmates traveled abroad for school, but I could not even think about that because my mom couldn't afford it. Once, my mom had asked her brother, who was abroad, to help get one of her children abroad, but that uncle told mom that it would be like climbing a very tall tree for this to happen. So, I pushed the idea out of my mind.

Going to School Abroad

I got admission to study biochemistry at the University of Nigeria, Nsukka (UNN). The first time I traveled there from Cameroon, we traveled by road, as my mom could not afford a flight for me. And even though many other students also took the road trip option, it was a rough ride. On the other hand, the trip was exciting as it was my first time out of Cameroon. I was going to live by myself, and that was something to look forward to. I was very expectant and excited about the new things to explore and experience.

When we got to UNN, I met my cousin, who was in his final year. He introduced me to his friends and a lot of other Cameroonians at school. He also scammed me out of some money before leaving with the pretext of keeping it for me. I blended in and made some friends, attended all the parties I could, and dated one of my cousins' friends, my first real boyfriend. Let me use this opportunity to discourage anyone from judging too quickly. Back in Cameroon, I regularly went to clubs, and anyone could have assumed I had been changing boyfriends like underwear. Still, the truth is, I never had any intimate relationship with any man until I went to school at UNN. Even this first boyfriend was surprised because looking at me, you would have thought otherwise. Never judge a book by its cover. We ought to learn from our heavenly Father, who looks at the heart and not the outward appearance.

I, the LORD, search the heart; I examine the mind to reward a man according to his way, by what his deeds deserve.
Jeremiah 17:10 NKJV

I had a group of four friends with whom I used to party a lot. Our Cameroonian community at school called us campus babes because we lived in the hostels on campus and would travel to other cities and states to go party. This behavior was not very safe in Nigeria because people were used for rituals in some places, but God kept us even amid this unsafe lifestyle.

A relationship with God was nowhere in the picture of my life, though. I remember going to a state four hours away from campus to visit a lecturer's friend in a village. This trip was a spur of the moment decision made by my three friends and me. We went on this trip and told none of our Cameroonian community friends that we were going. The house to which we went in this town called Umuahia was so beautiful and sophisticated. The rooms had phones and intercom to communicate with one another.

When the host saw us, he zeroed in on me; but I was not interested. He tried all night to persuade me to get intimate with him, but I wouldn't budge, as I didn't like how he looked at all. He promised me trips to different countries for vacation and other offers, but my mind was made up. This stance did not sit well with him, so the next morning, we headed back to campus instead of our initial plan to spend the whole weekend. With man, nothing comes free.

Later on, I had other relationships in Nigeria, and this brings to memory a guy I called uncle Sam. He was friendly and very polished. Whenever I was visiting him from campus, I would take my friends along. We called his house the fattening room because once we got there, he would feed us lavishly. Keep in mind that the campus was a desert, especially towards the end of the semester when all our money was gone.

God has always been with me. There was a time we were going back to school in Nigeria from Cameroon, and I decided to go by boat with my friends. My mother was opposed to the idea of a boat trip because of the scary stories of people getting lost and dying in the sea. But I was determined to go back to school via this route as it was faster; you got to Nigeria from Limbe, Cameroon, in under four hours, compared to the road trip, which took about two days on the bad roads on the Cameroonian side. Of course, flying was out of the question as it was sometimes even difficult for my mom to put together school fees and pocket money.

This boat trip with ten other students going back to school was not smooth. The boat engine failed, and we were stranded in the middle of the sea with no life jackets. We sat in the boat for about three hours, as seawater started getting into the boat with the rising tides. We were rescued when a fishing boat came by and took us to a fishing island close-by. We spent the night there, which was just as dangerous as being stranded in the water, as anything could have happened to us on that strange island. The next morning, another boat was found, which then took us to Nigeria. One would think this experience would be enough to deter me from using the boat, but it was not. God always protected me through those journeys, even though I didn't love God or think about Him.

I had this chemistry course that involved doing an internship, so I secured a position at the oil refinery in Limbe during one of my school breaks back in Cameroon. It used to be very difficult to get a job in this company, even as an intern, but through my mom's connections, I was able to get a place.

The experience was exciting, and I was able to earn some money myself. I met some of the workers, and one of the managers became interested in me. I started dating this guy though he was not single. You know, when you are a sinner, the devil can get you to do just about anything, and you will come up with numerous excuses to convince yourself that you are doing okay. I told myself I was just having fun because this manager would take me out to places I couldn't go by myself, and he also gave me money. His money and spending were all forgotten by the time the school break ended, and I was back to school.

There was this born-again Christian brother who kept preaching Jesus to us, but none of us paid him heed. One day, he was almost crying as he spoke to us. Now, I truly understand why and the passion that lay behind those tears. He knew that if anything had happened to us, then we were candidates for hell.

On Easter day of 1997, my last year in the university, we went to this little church, and when the pastor made an altar call for those who wanted to repent, I went out with some of my friends and accepted Jesus as my Lord and personal Savior. It was quiet and peaceful for about a month or two. We learned a song and sang it wherever we could, at parties, gatherings, and so on.

The lyrics of this song are:

♪ ♫ *How I love You! You are the one; You are the one! How I love You! You are the one for me.*

I was so lost but You showed the way, because You are the way I was so lost but You showed the way to me.

I was lied to but You told me the truth because You are the truth I was lied to but You told the truth to me.

I was dying but You gave me life, because You are the life I was dying but You gave Your life for me. ♫

The song is a beautiful one, but I forgot the lyrics too quickly and went back to my old ways, telling myself that the Christian life was boring. Of course, this was also a lie from the pit of hell. God is fascinating once you know Him and have a relationship with Him. He will teach you and keep you positively occupied because He has work for us all.

After graduation, I stayed at school six extra months after my classmates left because of a chemistry laboratory assignment that I had to redo. I don't know why this course was a problem for me; a course that was supposed to last for three years took me five years because of the many strikes and schools being shut down for months. But I finally made it and graduated with second class honors. With this, I went back home to Cameroon. Thank you, Jesus.

Graduation

Finally, I'm a graduate! Back home from Nigeria with a university degree, yes! Job? No. Sure, I went job hunting, but in Cameroon, if you don't have Godfathers or connections, there is very little chance of you getting a job. So, I was home with no job, wondering about what next step to take in life.

Then, I reconnected with the manager I dated years back at the oil company where I had my internship. He was no longer working for that oil company but wanted to start a consulting company in Cameroon's economic capital. When he asked me to come work with him, I was delighted and confident it was a bridge to wherever and whatever life had in store for me.

We resumed the abandoned relationship. The gentleman was married, but at that time, I didn't think much about his marital status. All that mattered was, he was making my life better than it was.

My life, thanks to him, was acceptable to my standards: eating out at expensive restaurants with some meals costing more than a month's salary to some people: night clubs, bars, casinos, and even a visit to a strip club at one time, an experience I did not like; so, I never went back. (Watching half-naked women dancing was not precisely a spectacle I enjoyed.) My life was just a mess. I made other friends who made this lifestyle enjoyable, always ensuring there was something to do or somewhere to go. 29I would occasionally go to church, the Winner's Chapel, but had no relationship with God and was not committed. I only went if I felt like it. One time, I tried to get serious but couldn't because it meant stopping the relationship I had with my 'Sugar Daddy Manager.' I could not imagine breaking from him because my life revolved around our relationship and, with it, the job. It seemed like bondage looking at it as a Christian now, but then it was a good life to me, especially in Africa.

Something supernatural happened to me, though, while I was attending that church. I went to church one Sunday, and a lady came and gave a testimony that God healed her in her dream. I used to have a toothache, and in my sin, I still asked God, "If indeed you healed this lady, then, take away my toothache also." And do you know that as I went to sleep that night, I dreamt some doctors worked on my teeth, and when I got up the next morning, the toothache was gone! I was shocked but happy, and I have never forgotten that dream.

Even in our fallen state and sin, God is still good to us. He healed me from the toothache, which would have cost me a lot of money had I gone to the dentist. This scripture comes to mind:

But God, who is rich in mercy, because of His great love with which He loved us, even when we were dead in trespasses, made us alive together with Christ (by grace you have been saved).
Ephesians 2:4-5 NKJV

Because of God's love for us, He still heals and protects us even in our sins. Since the healing, I have not had any dental work done.

Now, 'Sugar Daddy Manager' became serious and started talking about me being his second wife, which was never part of the plan. I started thinking of a way out, and school was the best option. One of my friends in England helped me gain admission into a school in England for accounting, which I later switched for a Master's in Information Technology.

While in school, I connected with a guy in the USA, and I told myself it was time to settle down because my biological clock was ticking fast. This relationship never worked out. Meanwhile, I was still dating the Sugar Daddy Manager in Cameroon. He would come for a vacation to France, and I would fly over from England to meet him. Sometimes, he would come to visit me in England. While at school, I tried coming on vacation to the US, but I wasn't granted a visa. I finally finished my Master's program, secured an internship in the US, and that was how I found myself in the United States.

I lived with my friend in Atlanta while on my internship. A mutual friend connected me to the guy who would be my daughter's father. He lived in Maryland. After communicating for a while, he came over to Atlanta to visit, and we started a relationship. Done with the internship, I decided to stay and sort myself out in the US and hopefully get married. I moved to Maryland and continued this relationship with my daughter's father, but it didn't work out. I got my beautiful daughter, though.

Whenever I brought up the topic of marriage during our relationship, it was always one excuse after another. When this man was not proposing, even with my pregnant state, many thoughts crossed my mind; top on the list was what my family would say about my terrible combination of being pregnant with no real job and no husband. But this voice told me to keep the baby; this was the first time I indeed heard the loud voice of God, despite my zero-relationship with Him. I had peace then and knew everything would be fine, no matter what, though I didn't know how.

Even after I had my baby, which my guy never wanted right from the onset, he still came up with excuses. So, I had to end the relationship, knowing it was taking me nowhere, and I had things to put right in my life. A little advice, ladies: If a man wouldn't marry you when you don't have a child for him, they would still not marry you even when you have one. So, don't keep yourself bound to a man who has a truckload of excuses in the place of marriage.

While living in Maryland, I occasionally attended a church, and one of my friends brought a flyer about a visiting pastor who was coming from Dallas to preach. I had just had my baby; she was about two months old. Pastor W. (later, Apostle W), the false prophet, was the visiting pastor on the church event flyer. I knew Pastor W. while in Africa. He was a family friend and entirely far from being a man of God; so, the flyer was surprising, and I promised to attend the program, if not for anything, but to see this miracle that God had wrought in his life. In Africa, he was more of a scammer and smooth talker.

I attended the program with my daughter and was nicely surprised because he preached very well and passionately. After the program, I met him and his wife, whom I also knew from back then, as a friend to my younger sister. It was a happy reunion after many years. I invited them to my house the next day, and we spent that weekend together. He asked me to consider moving to Dallas, but I refused as I still had things to sort out in Maryland. Recall that I just had my baby. I was thinking hard about how to take care of myself and my baby. One of my good friends told me of a nursingschool with the LVN program for 12 months, which I decided to attend. I took my baby to my sister in Ohio while I attended school and worked in Maryland. I was no longer alone but had a baby to raise alone since marriage was not coming from the direction of the baby's father. Life became more serious; partying and fooling around with no cares in the world came to a halt.

I finished LVN school quickly with valedictorian honors. I already had a Master's, and my first degree was in biochemistry, and those made it easy to perform excellently. Still, no job was coming my way. I started having issues in Maryland; so, I decided to leave Maryland. I thought about Pastor W's invite and took the move to Dallas as the next best thing. Seeing as nothing else was working in my life, it was time to get serious with God and let Him change my story and give me the peace that I desperately needed. I knew God was the answer to my problems after going round in circles for so many years with no headway.

Pastor W being a pastor now, after the life he previously led, really made me think about fully committing to God and be a true Christian. There must have been something about God, I was missing out on, and if Pastor W could turn to God, then it was high time I took a similar step. Mind you, in Africa, I thought being a Christian meant joining a cult. When two of my sisters became born-again Christians, I cried because I felt they joined a cult and the Christians I knew looked so broke. My sisters educated me, and when I went to Nigeria, I saw that Christianity was not at all what I thought, and people were actually happy and very successful being Christians.

So, I came to Dallas to really know God, love God, fully commit to Him and His ways, and to get all that I had been missing. I was finally ready. Pastor W. and his wife warmly welcomed me into their home. I started attending church with them. Soon enough, Pastor W asked me to join the choir, and I did, though I had never been in one before. I considered it a learning experience, and because I love singing, I went into it with all my heart. Rehearsals were never missed, and I ensured my weekends were free so that I could be at church. I was very committed.

From the little I saw the few times I attended church prior, the pastors' wives helped their husbands. I noticed Pastor W's wife was not very involved in the church; so, I encouraged her to do better, so she would not be left out in the church's going-ons and also have more common ground with her husband. This was 2008. The church grew from the storefront to buying its building, a significant milestone for the church. The new church was secured with generous member donations, and the church moved from the storefront to the new building.

The church was always very full; you had to come early to secure a good seat. I wasn't involved in leadership or administration of the church, except for the choir; so, I never knew what was going on behind the scenes after church or in the leadership. At home, my relationship with the Pastor's wife was excellent. She would complain about the husband at times, but I would comfort and tell her to forgive and just support him; for I believed being a pastor of a church of about three hundred members then took a lot of dedication and time. I lived with them for about six months and moved to my place after securing a job. I was happy at the church, and at surface value, everything looked right in the church.

My best friend from Maryland had moved to Dallas months before I did, and our partying continued. No one preached about holy living at church, so I thought the partying and clubbing were still okay. However, I noticed a waning interest in the parties. I was beginning to spend less time at the parties and would sometimes not even make it out of bed to attend after dressing up and deciding to take a nap. I would finally convince my friend that we did not have to go out. This continued until my friends started finding ways to exclude me from going out with them to avoid the inevitable; I spoiled their fun by either falling asleep on the closest chair right there in the club or asking to leave early. That was how I finally stopped clubbing and partying. On the other hand, I was always happy at church, in the presence of God, listening to His Word and worshipping. God was drawing me close to Him, unknown to me.

I got my daughter from my sister to come live with me since I was now stable. Pastor W had young daughters almost my daughter's age, so his wife suggested enrolling my daughter at the same school with their daughters, so she could help keep her after school since I would still be at work. I was very grateful for the arrangement at the time, even though it sometimes meant picking up my daughter late after work from the pastor's house. I thought Pastor W and his wife were okay with it and were my spiritual parents. I started calling the pastor's wife 'Mama' as a sign of respect for her being a mother to the church as the pastor's wife.

One day at work, I got a call from my daughter's school telling me I had three days to transfer my daughter to the school in her zone because I didn't live in the area where she was attending school. It was stressful for me, having to start thinking of who to keep her with after school, but I eventually worked out a solution with some of my friends, and we endured the arrangement until I moved from that location.

My Life at the Church

I continued serving in the choir and was very dedicated. It required no extra effort to be dedicated as I loved being a chorister. I loved the church family, and being a somewhat reserved person, I didn't know much of what happened after church services or behind the scenes. During my ten years in the church, I don't remember visiting another church because I was content in the church. There were a lot of church gatherings where people brought food, and everyone ate together.

    About 2012, one of the ladies at the church introduced me to her brother in Tanzania. We got talking about marriage until I visited him in Tanzania. Again, this relationship didn't work out either. I am a smart, beautiful woman and was curious why my relationships were not working out. But I never allowed this to bother me much.

At work, I met a fellow Cameroonian lady, and we became friends. I told her about my church. She finally started attending on someone else's invitation. She told me a lot about God speaking to her in dreams, but I wondered how this could be. I told her if God was speaking to her in her dreams, I also wanted to hear God speak to me. The next thing I knew, God started showing me things in my dreams; very vivid pictures. The excitement that came with this new experience was that I couldn't wait to sleep to dream.

A lot of people are ignorant because they lack knowledge. I did not go to church all my life, and the Bible was not one of the books I read. Maybe if things had gone a different way, I would have known early enough that God does speak to us via dreams and would have paid more attention to my dreams. When I finally learned so, I started paying attention to my dreams and writing some of them down in my dream book.

My people are destroyed for lack of knowledge. Because you have rejected knowledge, I also will reject you from being priests for Me; Because you have forgotten the law of your God, I also will forget your children.
Hosea 4:6 NKJV

A family joined the church from another state. This couple had seven children, and they didn't live very far from Pastor W's residence; and soon enough, the lady got quite close to the Pastor's wife. I never thought much of the relationship since the Pastor's wife related well with everyone at church.

One memorable Sunday at church, this new lady who

recently joined the church dropped a bombshell right at the pulpit. She took the microphone as though to give a testimony. Right there, in full view of the whole congregation, she announced that she had been having an adulterous relationship with the Pastor. Not stopping at the shocking revelation, she went into graphic details of what had transpired between them in the bedroom and how Pastor W had promised to take her to Canada to start a new life with her.

To say we were all shocked would be an understatement. I didn't believe her, along with some others, but another part of the church believed. The church was split, and a lot of people left. This lady and her husband sent emails to almost everyone at church with graphic details of the relationship and other things that the pastor had confided in her.

I could not bring myself to read the email. I was in great denial. Who could have imagined the pastor having an extramarital affair, not to mention with the married mother of seven kids? I came to church expecting to see something different from the world I left behind, to have peace and get to know Jesus and for Him to change my life and story, not this.

My old life had left me empty and wanting, and I had gotten tired of it. My search for a more fulfilling and better life led me to church and God. It was not supposed to end with me hearing that my pastor, who was supposed to lead me towards Christ and a better life, was cheating with a married woman.

I refused to believe the story, going further to send a text message to Pastor W reiterating my trust in him and absolute disbelief of the lady's account. I never asked him if she spoke the truth or lied. In my narrow mind, he couldn't have gone back to the life he led before coming to Christ. To me, that's like going back to Egypt, to bondage, to slavery.

Another pastor was invited the next Sunday to preach in an attempt to reassure people and restore order at the church. Services continued.

Then, a friend in church confided in me sometime later that the pastor was having an affair with another lady in the church who had confided in my friend. Again, I refused to believe her, thinking they just wanted to tarnish the pastor's name and image. While I kept the information at the back of my mind, I did not let these infidelity allegations bother me. Later on, I learned the 'new' relationship had been ongoing simultaneously with the married woman who had exposed him in church.

A visiting pastor from Paris, who was also called a prophet, came to preach sometime later, and when I went to the office to say hello after service, he held my hand and prophesied. He told me that he saw a duck sitting on my head. Knowledge of deep spiritual things, demons, or spiritual afflictions was not taught or preached at Pastor W's church, and they were things I had no strong fort in. I was like a blank white sheet of paper concerning deep spiritual matters.

The prophet told me I needed to do a three-day dry fast to get delivered, which I quickly agreed to. There was no way any duck was going to keep sitting on my head.

On the first day of the three-day fast, while I was driving to work, I asked God what happened to cause a duck to be sitting on my head. God showed me a vision, and like a movie on my windshield, God flashed an incident that happened when I was still about nine years old and had forgotten entirely up until that moment. Remember when I met those voodoo priests at my home after school with my parents and many other people? That was the scene that flashed. God is so amazing. I was screaming in my car, being the first time I had a vision. I was amazed.

During the fast, I also had some dreams, but a particular one stood out: three women in long white dresses were praying for me. I felt so peaceful after the dream. The prophet prayed for me after the three days of fasting. I don't know if anything happened after the prayers because much didn't change in my life, and years later, evidence came up that this prophet is false.

I can now say this prophet is false because he visited a second time, and I started having lustful thoughts about him and dreams of seeing him as my husband until I had to tell my pastor. At this time, the prophet was engaged to an innocent girl he met at church. I dreamt that he got engaged to another lady different from the current one, and it came to pass. He broke up with the girl at church and wanted to get engaged to the other girl, but that didn't work out either. False prophets are laced with lust, and when they come around you or pray for you, they transfer the spirit to you, and you start lusting after them. I now know that dreams of you sleeping with a man of God when you are not married to him or even when married to him is of the devil, and dark powers usually manipulate those dreams.

In 2014, Pastor W. announced in church that God had given him a vision to raise five ministers, and he invited anyone interested to register for the training. I wasn't interested, so I did not register. When I went to his office, though, he advised me to register for the class, and I accepted, telling myself that knowledge is never wasted and it would be an opportunity to get to know God more. More than five people registered for the class, but some people dropped out along the way, and it was just six of us left in the class.

Pastor W was a very good teacher of the Word. The classes were exciting, and all of us in the class said the salvation prayer. There was a class called demonology, after which I had to look through my house to throw out some things that I thought might have come from the wrong source. I threw out some expensive outfits I had gotten from India and Pakistan, and thinking about it now; I should have prayed over them instead of just casting them out.

The class was close-knit, but I realized some of the women were not so friendly towards me. It was strange, especially as some of them thought I had something more going on with Pastor W. The truth is, I was close to him only because of the history of our families, but with him dating some of the women in the class, though I wasn't aware at the time, it was hard for them not to suspect every other woman around him. It was baffling how a Pastor meant to be your spiritual father had no qualms sleeping with you, definitely not of God!

Pastor W excluded me from a class on learning to preach on the pulpit and preparing sermons. He gave no suitable response when I asked for an explanation. It hurt, and I somehow felt rejected from the rest of the class, but I didn't let this bother me too much. Besides, I was busy with my online Masters in Healthcare Informatics. Not participating in the preaching class was one less burden. I also now realize that these false prophets and teachers see the call of God upon your life even when you are not aware of it and try to make sure you never fulfill it.

My relationship with God was growing at this time. I could hear God and speak to Him. I had a dream concerning the church in which I saw a lot of people processing out of the church with things like charms and some traditional articles. When I got up, I didn't understand the dream, but I told the Pastor's wife about it and my friend Min Sandra. Now I know God was showing me that many things in that church were not of Him, and I needed to get out of the church. God's love for us is immense. He shows us things to increase our awareness of our surroundings. The question is, do we understand what he shows us and take the relevant actions? Our dreams are important. There is the need to pay attention to them and get someone we trust to know God to interpret it for us when we don't understand. God already showed me that the church I was in was evil, but I didn't understand the dream.

The mother of a friend died, so I called her to offer my condolences. This friend explained to me that her mother had gone into a coma for hours three days earlier. When she came out of it, she kept complaining, asking who brought her back to this place (earth and the hospital bed). The mother then explained that she had gone to a beautiful place, filled with joy and singing people, and she wanted to go back there.

As my friend was explaining this to me, the Spirit of God told me that the mother had been to heaven and that I should go to her wake keeping and ask everyone there that if they died today, just like the mother who died, would they be making heaven as the mother did? I resisted at first because here was God asking me to do precisely what Pastor W. had excluded me from doing in his special classes. I obeyed God and called my friend to ask for a little time slot at her mother's wake keeping to say something, of which she gladly said yes.

On the day of the wake-keep, I was a little nervous, but I delivered the message to about seven hundred people present at the wake with the Holy Spirit's help. Some people were surprised because they knew me as the party girl, not the preacher, but God changed my life for the better, and I loved it. I had peace and purpose at last. Pastor W looked very uncomfortable and somewhat ashamed when I told him I had preached at the wake-keep. He had intended to keep me away from preaching, but my Father in heaven knows how to redeem His children and put to shame the enemies of progress.

By late 2014, we were done with the ministerial classes, and the ordination was planned. Before the ordination, I spoke with the apostle, and he told me his wife didn't want me ordained; but that it was his decision and that he was still going to ordain me. I was surprised and wondered why Mama would make a statement like that, but I held my peace.

Then after church one Sunday, the pastor's wife took one of the ladies in the church from the leadership, and they asked me if we could have a conversation; with her not wanting me ordained in my mind, my curiosity was on a high. The pastor's wife told me she wanted me to address her as 'first lady,' thenceforth. With the ordination saga fresh on my mind, I got pissed. I asked her to show me where in the Bible, anyone was addressed as the first lady. I told both of them that if they wanted to give me hell, I knew how to give it right back. I walked out of the meeting. These ladies got so annoyed that they ran to the pastor to report what I did, but I paid them no mind. This is when I started getting distant from the pastor's wife, and I believe this was all manipulation by the pastor to separate me from the wife.

We were finally ordained. The ordination was surreal, a lot of men of God were invited, family members, and other visitors. During the ordination, another prophet prophesied that I would soon be married to a pastor and that the pastor would be one that had been in ministry for some time and not just any young and upcoming pastor. This prophecy never came to pass because I am still single, and it is five years since that declaration, and it makes me wonder if he got that prophecy from God.

After the ordination, a pastor was invited from out of state, American and Spirit-filled. During the service, one of the ministers received the baptism of the Holy Spirit and started speaking loudly in tongues. I also got the baptism of the Holy Spirit the same day, and I started speaking in tongues quietly but couldn't stop it. My teeth were chattering the whole of that day, and I had very little sleep that night as I spoke in tongues almost all night. My relationship with God got closer and stronger, and I could hear God more.

I was still in the choir, and as I led praise and worship one Sunday, the move and presence of the Holy Spirit was strong in the congregation. People started crying in the church, and some spoke in tongues. But after service, Pastor W met me and told me that indeed my worship brought God's presence during the service, but I shouldn't let it get to my head. This came as a surprise, but I kept quiet, wondering what he meant by that.

At this point, it was obvious Pastor W. never wanted me to grow spiritually. I started having many dreams, and when I would tell him some of my dreams, he would say to me I dreamt too much and discouraged me every opportunity he had. A dream I had after my ordination: some people were throwing balls of fire at me, but I flew above them and sent back the fire to them, telling them,

> *"He that is in me is greater than he that is in the world"*
> *(1 John 4:4).*

So, they ran back to the lady, sending them that they couldn't bring me down or capture my heart. I got from the dream that the witches were angry; I now belong to God and have a relationship with Him; they had wanted to stop me.

You are of God, little children, and have overcome them, because He who is in you is greater than he who is in the world.
1 John 4:4 NKJV

    A few months later, the pastor started the pursuit, the predator hunting for its prey right at church. God had shown me in a car with a man in an earlier dream, and I saw Jesus ahead of us. The man in the car, instead of driving towards Jesus, started driving away from Jesus and Jesus became smaller and smaller as he drove away, I was telling him to drive towards Jesus; that it was Him I was looking for, but he didn't heed my voice, and I woke up from the dream. Now I know the man in the car was Pastor W; instead of taking me towards Jesus, he took me away from Jesus.

    We have to seek the face of God before going into any church; and should not allow sentiments to cloud our judgment. That church might be a voodoo house, not a church; and instead of getting to know Jesus, they take you further away from Him.

My Entanglement with Pastor W., the False Prophet

I lived with Pastor W. and his family for six months, and he sometimes took me out for dinner or lunch, this was how close I was to the family. I considered him my spiritual father and was very open with him. Being my cousin's friend, I also considered him a friend.

But after driving a wedge between his wife and me, Pastor W started confiding in me about his marital issues and frustrations. I advised him as best as I could, being unmarried myself, but I soon realized this was all a plot to get me to sympathize with him. He complained about his unloving and wicked wife and the constant albeit unsuccessful struggle to fix the marriage.

On one occasion, he was invited to minister in France with his wife, but she refused to go with him because he had to continue from there to Africa, and the wife would have had to return alone to the US. This incident seemed to corroborate some of the complaints, so I started feeling sorry for him.

One evening, he took me out to dinner, and after dinner, we went to a park bench and started conversing. As we were leaving, he hugged me, which was not out of place. But mid-hug, I felt his manhood smack in the center of my stomach. I was taken aback and shifted away as fast as I could in my shocked state. I ignored it, said nothing, and decided to assume it meant nothing and continued as if nothing happened.

But on getting home, I was bothered about the possibility that my pastor had been thinking sexually about me. In one of our numerous discussions, I told him I would never date anyone close to my brothers or cousins. That aside, he was a married Man of God and, to top it all, my spiritual father, pastor, and mentor.

According to him, the lady who stood on the pulpit to talk about the affair with him went crazy because she lied about him, and he referred to the scripture, "Touch not my anointed and do my prophets no harm." I know better now that he attacked her spiritually with voodoo for exposing him.

> *"Do not touch My anointed ones, and do My prophets no harm."*
> *Psalms 105:15 NKJV*

Not too long after that, the pastor invited me to dinner. Ignoring what had transpired weeks earlier, I accepted the invitation. Dinner was at a nice Mediterranean restaurant with private booths. He ordered wine with our food, and not being a big drinker, I had very little.

We were done eating and were talking when he took my hand towards him and placed it on his thigh. Where I thought I'd meet the fabric of his trouser, I instead felt bare, warm flesh. At that moment, I realized Pastor

W. had taken advantage of the booth being private to unzip himself. I am confident my shock and repulsion were registered clearly on my face. At this point, the desperation of this married Man of God to get into a sexual relationship with me seemed totally out of the ordinary.

When I got home, I spent the whole night crying out to God; I told God that Pastor W was His servant and He should be the one to deal with him. And God answered. The next morning, Pastor W called me to say that my father visited him the previous night and warned him to stay off me. At first, I didn't understand what he meant. Then, remembering how I criedout to God all night, I felt some peace, thinking he would honor what God told him and leave me alone.

A statement the pastor made after his encounter with God that I did not pay much attention to, was that he never knew God was in the church. I understand better now because Pastor W was not serving God; so he assumed he was insulated from God. This should have been a warning sign for me, but I let it slide.

Pastor W. didn't give up on his pursuit. To make things worse, what happened in the booth messed my mind. I started thinking a lot about him sexually and lustfully. It is my belief that his intention was to plant the seed of lust in me. I started getting distracted during his preachings at church. It never even occurred to me that I could leave the church.

Finally, the intimacy started. If I remember correctly, he came to my house while my daughter was at school. Out of respect for him, I opened my door when he came knocking. Of course, he and his family were regular visitors at my house; so, his presence was not supposed to be weird, except for the recent events. We got talking, and one thing led to the other, and we found ourselves in bed.

Afterward, I felt so bad. I thought of our families and the effect it would have on them if people found out. I told him it was a mistake that should never repeat itself. I felt violated, not that I was raped but because he violated the trust I had in him as my spiritual father and friend.

I cried out to God and asked Him to forgive me. God forgave me and gave me the scripture of the woman caught in adultery, "Go and sin no more." I felt a little better, thinking that was the end of it. But it was not. It felt like we had been immersed in the spirit of lust and the relationshipwent on for more than a year. The relationship was like a burden on my shoulders as I had to hide it from everyone.

She said, "No one, Lord." And Jesus said to her, "Neither do I condemn you; go and sin no more."
John 8:11 NKJV

I remember asking Pastor W, "How can you go to the pulpit every Sunday and still have an intimate relationship with me?"

His reply was, *"You can have two separate lives, one for the church and one out of the church."* Such duplicity was a rude shock for me.

This was my pastor sinning and telling me it was okay. What of the commandments? Could it be that, "Do not commit adultery" and do not fornicate meant nothing to him? Was it possible that those instructions did not exist in his Bible?

I have no recollection of anyone even preaching against sin or encouraging holy living at the church. This is also a sign of false church; holiness should be preached at church, for God wants us to be holy just as He is Holy, and without Holiness, no one can see God.

I was still in the choir and singing. I felt like a fraud, but I couldn't get out of the relationship. I felt like I was under a spell. Sometimes, I would fight hard and tell him when he called, that he was distracting me; and that I wanted to spend time with God. He would hang up only to call back in a short while. He persisted till I started getting further and further away from God and more into the relationship. I came to church seeking to know God, love God, have some peace of mind, and a deeper relationship with God, but I found myself going back to the pit I was in when I was in the world.

Sometimes, I truly felt bad for God, if that was possible, for all the mess going on in His church. Our God is loving and merciful, and even in our sins, He loves and protects us. I was kind of protected in this relationship, or worse would have happened to me. This was the one time in my life that I wished I was a man. That way, this pastor would not have bothered me or stolen my peace. I started asking

God to lead me to a female pastor, and that finally happened years later.

During our relationship, I had asked Pastor W about the lady my friend told me he dated, if the story was true, especially now that he was having a relationship with me. He initially denied it but later confirmed it. I wondered about the other things he might have lied about, like this rumor about having a daughter with his sister-in-law.

Most of the church ladies were 'babes' to him, and he always told them he loved them. The majority of them were already lusting after him, and some of them were single and saw this as a green light to start developing feelings for him. When I pointed this out to him, he just told me he loved everybody. But I knew it was a deliberate act to get them lusting after him and unable to reject him when he came unto them.

At church, the ordained ministers were given new positions, and I became the minister in charge of finances. Now I started wondering that if Pastor W. was having an affair with me, he could have affairs with other church ladies. He was always telling me how the ladies at church had erotic dreams about him. In this same church, a lot of the ladies dressed seductively already. I started thinking of all the complaints his wife had been making about him; it was just a total mess.

Why should the women at your church be having erotic dreams of you or even think about you sexually? It just never sounded right to me. I thought he was exaggerating, but apparently, he was not. He had passed on the spirit of lust to everyone. There was this very assertive minister. She wanted to take over almost everything at church and was acting like the mama of the church. I drew the pastor's attention to her, trying to make him see she could only do that if he permitted her. But he denied ever encouraging her in that way or having a relationship with her. I dropped it. God showed me in a dream that Pastor W and the minister were having an affair; and confronting him with the dream too, he denied it again, and I let it slide once again. One of the female ministers left the church suddenly and would not speak to anyone at the church. That puzzle was never solved. At home, the pastor's marriage was not going well, and his wife even stopped coming to church for almost a year.

Pastor W started talking about divorcing his wife. But this was just one of his guises to get you to believe he wanted to marry you. He would say she was never the woman for him, and he never loved her. Honestly, I felt sorry for the wife but was handicapped to stop my affair with him. In all of these, the pastor kept confiding in me, telling me of his escapades and adventures. One of them was about a lady he cheated with who used to be the choir leader at the church until she got pregnant and left. He also confided in me that this choir leader aborted the pregnancy, and he gave her money for the abortion.

Some things became clear to me: the Pastor had a problem that needed taking care of - his constant infidelity and blame-shifting on the lack of love in his marriage. I now understand that sex is worship to the devil, which explains why false prophets are always sleeping around, giving worship to the devil their master.

One day, out of the blues, Pastor W told me about sleeping with a mother and daughter who had earlier attended the church. I was shocked and rattled, unable to wrap my head around the audacity to do such a thing and talk about it. He claimed it was the lady's daughter that threw herself at him. When I challenged him regarding his role and responsibility as the spiritual father to correct, reprimand, and protect this lady even if it meant him fleeing with his pants down, he had no reply. I became distant for some weeks, but I forgave him later on. There is just so much evil going on in churches infested with false prophets, and that is why God wants us to expose them.

"And have no fellowship with the unfruitful works of darkness, but rather expose them."
Ephesians 5:11 NKJV

Pastor W proposed a blood pact to seal our love for each other forever. How could a sensible Man of God with knowledge of spiritual things think like this? Whatever was between us was going nowhere forward; asking for a blood pact was totally off point. But he knew exactly what he was doing. He thought me very naive concerning spiritual things, and really, I was, to some extent, but not on this one. Even in the world, I knew the seriousness of any blood pact. We never made the blood pact; I just ignored the statement.

He wanted to set deep, spiritual bondage of keeping me trapped to him and unavailable to other men for marriage. Then I had a dream of getting married to him, and sometimes he would sleep with me in my dreams. I attributed it to the ongoing affair. But, spiritually, he had married me.

Later, I learned that I could never marry if that spiritual marriage was not broken. I contemplated a lot about including this in this book, but I am led to. This is so that anyone reading this book is aware of what is going on in these voodoo houses called 'churches' being run by false prophets and for the victims to regain freedom.

Then, I became pregnant. In my heart, I had decided to keep the baby despite the commotion it was bound to bring. But Pastor W came to my house and threatened me to abort it. I finally did, and he paid for it. That night, I wept and crawled on the floor, asking God to forgive me. God did forgive me, and I felt free from that guilt.

This pastor had also impregnated the little girl, with whom he had an affair with the mother and daughter. The mother was also under the evil spell, and when he found out, he had made them abort the pregnancy. An opportunity came up for the mother to expose Pastor W to another lady, but he once again manipulated the situation to his advantage. He used me as a tool to silence this woman by telling me what had happened and telling me to ask the mother, which made her afraid that I might expose what had happened to her and her daughter. False prophets would use you as their snitch to send or get information concerning others, and blindly, you would do their bidding, unknowingly becoming a part of their evil team.

Later, I learned that false prophets do not use protection to get the ladies pregnant and then terminate the pregnancies as a form of sacrifice to their master, the devil. False prophets are evil. They care for no one and love only themselves. Run far away from them. They are also very manipulative.

The pianist's wife just came from Nigeria with her children and joined the choir. At that time, she didn't have a car, so I helped her get to church and back. I have no idea what happened, but the wife started accusing me of being too close to her husband. I inquired as to what could have prompted such a statement. She told me I was making eye contact with her husband, the pianist, during praise and worship that Sunday service. For crying out loud, I was leading praise and worship that Sunday. How else was I to communicate with the pianist to change the music?

I was livid. I had one sinful relationship I was struggling with already and now, being accused of another affair with the pianist was just too much for me. I let loose all my frustrations on her. She went straight to Pastor W, who knew I was angry but hid behind the mess to deflect suspicions from his direction. A meeting was called, and some elders were invited to resolve the problem. The meeting didn't go well as I would not listen to anyone and walked out of the meeting.

Later, I calmed down and apologized to the lady. And while putting up a fatherly, disciplinary role on the outside, the pastor secretly apologized to me by telling me he knew nothing was going on between the pianist and me, but he had to resolve the situation. I was suspended from the choir for a month, but that was just for show on the pastor's side to prove he still had control.

I loved to praise God but was happy to be out as I was getting tired of the double life. I still believed that Pastor W was a Man of God who just needed deliverance from his weakness. I suggested to him once to go for deliverance from the spirit of lust that was making him sleep around withwomen, but to my shock and amazement, he responded, "what if I love my sin?" I was speechless; he was unrepentant and loved his sin.

Once Pastor W was traveling and borrowed nine thousand dollars from me. He had told me he was waiting for some money he would receive in two months. I didn't have the money in cash, so I told him I would get it from my credit card, and he would refund it in two months. Two months came and went by, and it was one excuse after another. Only about two thousand five hundred dollars could be gotten back from him. He scammed me as he did many of the women at church, claiming he didn't have to say, " God said," but only had to ask.

I believe he was sleeping with most of these women he was always asking for money from and using their credit cards. Our God is a giver, not a taker. Our God is orderly and does not wish for us to be found wanting. During Pastor's appreciation that year, I refused to give the pastor any gift because he owed me money; and I said to myself that I would honor him with his gift when he refunded my money. The Pastor was not happy about it because other ministers contributed.

But God didn't let me rest. When I got back home, He told me I was supposed to 'give honor to whom honor is due' and at the right time, not when it was convenient for me. So, I had to rectify the situation. Even in that mess, God was still putting an order in the church and nudging me to do what was right.

Pastor W gave me many hints to show me he was a false pastor, but I did not see them because I believe I was under a spell. The money was never enough at church; sometimes, the leadership had to chip in cash for the mortgage to be paid.

Then Pastor W became ordained as an Apostle. The

full ordination looked very weird to me, especially considering that he was with me the night before and we were not praying. He came to my house dressed in all black and almost drunk, not in the Holy Ghost but with alcohol. When I asked him where he was coming from, he said from a meeting. What kind of meeting got you all drunk the night before your ordination? I wondered... Definitely not a Christian meeting.

During the Ordination, I just sat watching and thinking. This man was with me last night, almost drunk with alcohol, and had committed adultery that very night. When did he repent of his sins or cleanse himself? I just felt so sorry. All through the ceremony, I was speaking with my heavenly Father, asking for His forgiveness. There was so much sickness in the church, all the sin, deep undercurrents of tension amongst the women, but I couldn't help myself by leaving the church. I believe now, I stayed on from the spell and loyalty that the spell demanded because I knew now that he was sleeping with other women at the church.

But God reminded me of the scripture that said Jesus came to heal the sick, not the healthy, and the church was a place for sick people. I pray you never find yourself in any such churches where instead of getting healed, you worsen. It is a nightmare come true as it is better to not identify as a Christian than to call yourself one and go through all this; the guilt is too much.

When Jesus heard it, He said to them, "Those who are well have no need of a physician, but those who are sick. I did not come to call the righteous, but sinners, to repentance."

Mark 2:17 NKJV

Pastor W. wore this ring and cross-chain at the ordination, and I assumed it was part of the things that apostles were ordained with.

He went to Florida for a program with some ministers from the church, including the lady minister I had dreamt he was having an affair with. He couldn't take me, probably because it could have been too hot for him. On his return, he was telling me how successful the program was and how he prophesied. I had never seen him prophesy, and he had always said he was not a prophet. He told me his prophecies were so accurate until a lady in the program said to him that if he took off his ring, he would not be able to prophesy anymore. He said he just laughed at the lady. This statement was yet another hint that I missed.

Apostle W loves fame and honor, just like any other false prophet. When his nephew came back from serving in Afghanistan, the nephew and his colleagues did a thanksgiving service at the church, and Apostle W invited one of the television news stations to record the event. He got himself attached to the Mayor of Grand Prairie and sometimes would go pray when they had their meetings, and some of the ministers at church would go with him. At some point, he was even talking of running for a position at the Mayor's office. Just like BarJesus, the false prophet in the Acts of Apostles who got himself attached to the proconsul so he could gain some influence. It was all about the show, the fame, the honor, and the power—nothing about leading people to Christ or getting them to love God.

Our affair continued, and still, I was glued to the church like a chair and couldn't get out.

A friend who lived next door to me, now a minister,

attended Apostle W's church but moved on to another church with a female pastor. I asked God to show me a sign to leave the church, but I got no signal. One day, I prayed to God to show my friend if I should leave the church or not. The next day I contacted my friend and asked her if she had any dreams. She said yes and that in the dream, she saw me and Apostle W. standing by the wayside. This didn't help me because I didn't understand the dream, but I was happy God showed her the dream. It confirmed that God still heard my prayers.

In 2016, my friend invited me to a vigil at her church. I didn't want to go, but I forced myself to attend. This heavy burden the relationship with the Apostle had placed on my shoulders weighed so much on me that I couldn't even share it with my friend. At the all-night prayer meeting, her pastor, who is a prophetess, prophesied to me. This is part of the prophecy in her exact words:

"You are stepping but not all the way God says do not half-step but go all the way for Him

As you go all the way for God, there is a wide-open door ahead of you, if you don't half-step

Don't do things to please anybody, pastor, friends; do things to please God. There is a full door that is open in front of you.

There is a heavy load on your back that God is removing from you. God wanted you to be here tonight for a reason; because He wants to take that load off from you. Go further; there is a wide-open door.

A new car, good things, but God wants you to go further, take more giant steps for God. God is taking that cork from your ears so you can hear more things spiritually, speaking in tongues."

When I got this prophecy, I was so happy and relieved. I was also amazed that God still thought me WORTHY to do His work, BE HIS SERVANT, despite the entanglement I found myself in. What a Merciful God! Also, my ears had been bothering me, and since the ordination, there was a restlessness within me to do more for God, but I didn't know what. I was also pleased that God would help me stop the illicit affair with the apostle. This came to pass, though it came a year later.

I watch Daystar a lot, a Christian Television channel, and I got some consolation from a pastor who came on to confess that she had had an extramarital affair for almost a year and a half, and God helped her to come out of it. This brought hope to my heart.

Sometime in 2017, one of my friends told me about the pain she had been having in her stomach for years, despite visiting many doctors and even having surgery. I still thought the Apostle was a servant of God, albeit flawed, so I invited my friend to come over so he could pray for her. The Apostle had told us stories about him praying for a lady who was almost dying, and she got healed. And even though such a miracle never happened at the church while I was there, I believed him. My friend came over but still got no relief. A visiting prophetess to our church from Las Vegas gave me a personal prophecy saying she saw me preaching to the nations. While at church, she prophesied that God had given me the gift of healing, but I never prayed for anyone because I didn't know. She encouraged me to start using the gift by praying for people.

So, I told Apostle W about this prophecy of me preaching to nations, but he tried to discourage me and make me forget about it; but I held on to my prophecy. Then my friend Min. Sandra sent me a video of a woman of God telling how she cast out shrines out of a lady. I was intrigued. I told myself I would like to meet this lady. The story she was telling sounded like what I read in the Bible about Jesus casting out demons; something I never saw at Apostle W's church.

I got interested and started watching this woman of God on Facebook. She is currently my Woman of God, Evangelist Belema Abili of Princess Belemzy Ministries. She is always on Facebook, preaching on loving and obeying God. I connected to her and have never stopped watching. A couple of weeks into watching her, she preached on how genuine love for Jesus makes you obey His commands and stop sinning. That got me as I thought of my relationship with the Apostle. I decided that I would end it, and I DID with the help of her videos, praying and asking God to help me; and I had some deliverance sessions. I wanted to love God and get to know him more.

I started watching her videos in late July 2017, and in early October, I got the leading to start preaching on Facebook. While watching her one day, it was as if God was speaking directly to me. She said, "If God tells you to do something, do it immediately. What are you waiting for?"

My friend, Minister Sandra, had been encouraging me to start preaching on Facebook, but I didn't because I wasn't sure if that was what God wanted for me. I also remembered the prophecy I had that God wanted me to do more for Him, so the evangelist's words became my confirmation. I did not mention it to the Apostle before I started preaching on Facebook. When I eventually did, rather than be happy for me and encourage me to do the work of God as any spiritual father should do, he got agitated.

He asked me why I even started when in three months, I was going to stop. I was not very surprised because he had never encouraged me with anything concerning God. What he had done instead was draw me farther away from God. He even had a meeting with the other ministers complaining about me, that I was the last person he would have thought would do something like that without informing him. I believe he thought I could never come out of the cage he had put me in. But I was not deterred. I continued preaching on Facebook and still do.

One Sunday service, right on the pulpit, he condemned the people who preached on Facebook, saying that it was not a real church. But this man never let me preach on his pulpit, so why was he so angry about me having my platform to preach the word of God? I figured it was all about control and gain as he couldn't control what I did or said on my platform, and whatever reward I might have from preaching on Facebook, he couldn't control or take credit for it. The day he finally asked me to preach at Bethel, God gave a message on choosing between life and death in (Deuteronomy 30:15-16),

> *"See, I have set before you today life and good, death and evil, In that I command you today to love the Lord your God, to walk in His ways and to keep His commandments, His statutes, and His judgements, that you may live and multiply, and the Lord your God will bless you in the land which you go to possess."*
>
> *Deuteronomy 30:15-16 NKJV*

Before the service, Apostle W asked me what I was going to preach on. When I told him, he said I couldn't preach such a message while he was in church. I never knew messages were chosen based on who was going to be present at the service. It was just his guilty conscience eating at him. He never asked me to preach again, telling me that my membership of the choir meant I was ministering all the time.

He once asked me why I was watching Evangelist Princess Belemzy, claiming he had listened to her and that my Bible knowledge surpassed that of the evangelist. For me, that was not the issue. The anointing was what mattered to me. Apostle W knew the Bible, but there was no anointing nor power in his messages. The word of God even tells us the kingdom of God is not in word but in Power, which apostle W never had except for his occultic powers. He knew I would get my deliverance from watching the evangelist and wanted to discourage and stop me.

For the Kingdom of God is not in word but in power.
1 Corinthians 4:20 NKJV

I was in an illicit relationship with him for almost two years and couldn't come out. Still, after listening to the Evangelist and following her on Facebook, I was able to stop the relationship in just about two weeks. I got delivered from a spiritual husband I never knew of and deliverance from many other things that I didn't even know I had.

Up to date, I still get deliverance while watching the WOG Princess Belemzy and staying connected. After ten years of staying at the false prophet's church and having an affair with him, multiple layers of evil have been deposited in me that need to come out.

I attended the Evangelist's birthday in October of 2017 and brought back some deliverance CDs. I gave them to a lady at church to listen to and get her deliverance. She did get her deliverance, but the Apostle heard of it and was angry. He asked me why I brought something that would not bethere when people started looking for it. The apostle cared for and loved no one but himself. If it didn't favor him, then it should not be done.

Early 2018, the evangelist announced she was planning to hold a program in Dallas. While still in bed one morning, the Holy Spirit asked me to tell her that our church was available if she wanted to hold the program at our church. At first, I resisted, thinking it was merely my thoughts, but I couldn't rest. So, I asked the Apostle if it was okay to rent the church since we were already renting it out to others. He said yes. On informing the WOG, she told me that she almost canceled the program for Dallas because all the venues found were costly, and she had just been praying to God to provide a venue when my message came in. God is awesome!

The program held and was powerful: many miracles, healings, and deliverance were witnessed. She also prayed for me to be anointed to do God's work, and I received it. Apostle W also attended the program and even refunded the five hundred dollars that the WOG paid for the venue, saying God told him to refund the money. I believe he was also trying to build some connections with the WOG.

Before evangelist Princess Belemzy prayed for me, I used to preach on Facebook without praying for people. After the prayers, I started praying for people to get their healing and deliverance. I posted the testimonies on Facebook, and I am sure the Apostle was surprised because some of the people I prayed for were members of his church, and some had spiritual spouses.

One night, just after I started preaching on Facebook, in my dream, a ball of air came into me through my private part right into my head, and I heard a voice saying, "You want to expose me." The air was like this breeze in my head that would start blowing whenever I began praying or worshipping God. I thought it was the witch in my family, who was discovered, earlier wanting to stop me from doing the work of God, but it was Apostle W who sent that evil arrow at me because he did the same to the other lady Minister. This sensation was a very uncomfortable attack from the enemy. Your enemies are those very close to you. The Word of God says your enemies are those of your household (Matthew 10:36).

And a man's enemies will be those of his own household.
Matthew 10:36 NKJV

My aunt, who always pretended to love everyone in the family, was pointed out as a family witch by a prophet who came from Nigeria to hold a program in Dallas. That night, she came and attacked me as I had been suspecting her. She always called at about midnight when I was sleeping, and that got me wondering. So, I asked my friend Minister Sandra to pray with me so she could be exposed if she was a witch; and not up to twenty-four hours later, she was exposed. Our God is awesome and powerful. God protected me; she couldn't do anything that night except send evil arrows that went right back to her.

This aunt is a friend to Apostle W. I asked how he

could be friends with a witch for so long and be a servant of God and not know. He quoted the Bible that God doesn't reveal everything to his servants (2 Kings 4:27). In this case, though, I believe he knew something because I blocked off this witch from my life, but he wanted to reunite us back. They are birds of a feather.

Apostle W. once asked me what I thought of the cult Rosicrucian. I could not even fathom why I would be thinking of a devilish cult I wanted nothing to do with; how much more by a man of God who should know better. My friend already told me of rumors hinting at Apostle W being a member of that cult. This still didn't register in my head as it should have, and I let it slide again. There was also the funeral of a medical doctor who was acclaimed to be a Rosicrucian. It is said that every member of the cult must be laid to rest by a fellow member of the cult present at the funeral. This medical doctor was laid to rest by Apostle W.

Apostle W also confided in me once that one of his fellow pastor friends was found one night at his church pulpit doing voodoo and chanting. He talked about it as if he would never do such, but he never exposed this pastor and continued being friends with him. The scripture that says 'not to have anything to do with the unfruitful works of darkness but expose them' meant nothing to the Apostle.

He also had this Ghanaian pastor friend who had suggested a ritual so that the church could be full. I would not know if he ever went for the ritual, but he is still friends with both pastors; and if birds of a feather flock together, it means he is one of them. God even taught us that anyone associated with a false prophet is also a suspect.

In the exposure of false prophets, we saw a video of

one who repented and described the things they did to get their powers as false prophets, including trips to India and Ghana to get charms. Apostle W had traveled to both of these places. His journey to India was not for any crusade or program; it was just to 'visit.' There were so many little details that I overlooked.

Some months after I started preaching on Facebook, Apostle W called me and invited me to lunch. I agreed and asked him to pick me up. When he came around, I was carrying out deliverance on a lady via phone. I was in my bedroom, releasing the Holy Ghost fire on her, so my daughter opened the door for him. I expected that he would wait for me to be done to go for lunch, but he left immediately. I called to ask why he could not wait a few minutes; he said he saw I was busy.

I went to meet him at the restaurant, and after we were done eating, he asked me when we were going to restart the relationship. My reply was that I now pray for people and cast out demons, not invite them into my life by sinning again. This man did not love or fear God. Sinning was a lifestyle for him, not an error to repent of. It then dawned on me that he could not wait while the deliverance session was going on at my house because the Holy Ghost fire was burning him, and he could not withstand it.

Apostle W visited Ecuador in South America a couple of years back for a crusade. With what I now know, I have wondered what God he was praying to during that crusade. He came back with an account of a boy who was afraid to come close to him, saying that the power he had was much greater than the power the boy had. What force had the boy seen in him? The marine and occultic powers?

In early 2018, the pastor he visited in Ecuador came to visit the church along with some other pastors. We had a wonderful time as the visiting pastor was a man of God who truly loved God. During this period, I had a dream to give Apostle W some money. I didn't even have money for my child's lunch but was restless till I gave him $250. When I gave him the money after the Sunday service the visiting pastors attended, he said he needed money to make a barbecue for the visitors and that it was indeed God who prompted me to give him the money.

I was happy when I obeyed what I saw in the dream, but now, I wonder if my dream was not manipulated. At the barbecue, the leader of the visiting pastors gifted me a scarf, which came as a pleasant surprise. Apostle W made the observation that I was the only one given a scarf and expressed his pleasure. But he was only trying to manipulate me.

He told me later that the pastor had decorated me with the scarf the moment I got to the barbecue because God had said I was supposed to be his wife and that his marriage to his current wife was in error. His plan was for me to restart the illicit affair we had before. The next day, he still came to my house to ask why I didn't want to cheat with him, that God already knew we were married in the spirit. I told him no, it made no sense to keep up anything with him until the real marriage happened, which I knew was never going to.

He kept spinning lies all in the bid to get me back in bed with him. God is not an author of confusion. You cannot have a wife at home, and He would tell you someone else should be your wife. It's a lie from the devil. When false prophets sleep with you, they steal the spiritual gifts God has given you, steal your anointing, deposit evil in you, cage you, and make you stagnant in everything you do. For the ten years I was in Bethel church; I saw no improvement in my salary. I completed a Master's in Healthcare Informatics and had three job interviews but could not secure a job. I know I am not dumb or lacking in skills; no, it was all due to the cage I was in.

In mid-2018, Minister Sandra left her church and came back to Bethel. We started doing little healing and deliverance programs at the church. One deliverance we did on a lady manifested a demon that said there was a marine spirit at the church and a red flag on the church. We wondered where that came from, so we told the Apostle that the church needed deliverance. He asked us to pray but went behind us to suggest to other pastors at church that he was not sure of the spirit Min. Sandra carried since she just came from another church.

I became the leader of the intercessory group at church. We decided to come early to church Sunday mornings to intercede before the service, going round the church premises to sprinkle the blood of Jesus. But the Apostle didn't want this, so he sent one of his pastors to come to interfere while he sat behind the scenes. He would very encouragingly tell us to do whatever we needed to do during the prayers while he was actively working to frustrate our efforts in secret. It was just so much confusion.

Apostle W also started a school in 2018 to train ministers just like we were trained in 2014. While we were praying in one of the classes, a lady started manifesting. We all prayed for her, and she became calm. But Apostle W made a statement in class that if I wanted, I could go to the streets and pray for all the witches but not in his class. After class, Min. Sandra and I decided to pray for that lady so she could get her complete deliverance. The Apostle saw us and interrupted the prayers, saying we could not do it there, it being a school, and he didn't want to be liable if anything should happen to the lady. The Apostle cared for no one but himself, and I believe he didn't want the lady delivered. I noticed there were some undercurrents and tension among the ladies in the class. It did not take long to realize the apostle had started his pursuit with the ladies in the new class. The minister he was dating (though he denied this) was also in the class. She finally left the school and the church, and I was curious as to what happened.

Some of the ladies attending the school started attending the Bethel church also. One of them preached on a Sunday and started talking about people being in the wrong marriages, and immediately I knew the Apostle had gotten to her also because this was the same line he used with me. I warned the Apostle not to deceive this woman as he did the minister that left the church.

Then I saw the minister who left the church, attending one of the Evangelist's deliverance programs on her Facebook live streaming. On December 31st, I invited her to attend the 24 hours program organized by the Evangelist to spend some time with her. I learned a lot of things concerning the Apostle from her. She told me Apostle W was in a cult; he had slept with her sister when she visited from Cameroon; and yes, he impregnated his sister-in-law and paid child support. He also reported to the school my daughter was attending with his daughters that it was not her school zone, which had made me move my daughter to another school, making us stressed about after-school arrangements.

The Apostle had also told her I would never get

married and only started preaching on Facebook searching for a husband; and that my ministry would never prosper. This raw wickedness and hatred was a lot to take in. I still had a little doubt, but I left the church then and never went back there or to the school.

I am searching for Jesus, not to join a cult, and I already had a prophecy that I would leave the church unexpectedly, and it just came to pass.

I finally told Min. Sandra that most of the things the lady minister said were true and confessed that the Apostle also had an affair with me. I am sure Minister Sandra was shocked, but she said nothing. The lady minister said nothing about her having a relationship with Apostle W, but I knew she had one; and I could sense that she was in so much pain and hurt. I felt sorry for her; her marriage was broken.

Many people at church were surprised that I left, knowing I had supported this man for ten years, denied all that was said about him, and kept believing that he just had a weakness and needed deliverance. I got many calls, but I just told everyone that my time at the church was over. I blocked Apostle W so that he couldn't reach me. I also called a lady I had invited to Bethel church to stop, as I had just got confirmation that the Apostle was not a man of God.

I was a young Christian who was ignorant and naïve concerning deep spiritual things. This kind of state makes us easy targets for these false prophets. Unfortunately, even those with in-depth spiritual knowledge can also be deceived because the false prophets are very cunning and use charms and spells. The Word of God tells us that false prophets will deceive even the elect of God (Matthew 24:24-25).

> *For false Christs and false prophets will rise and show great signs and wonders to deceive, if possible, even the elect. See, I have told you beforehand.*
> *Matthew 24:24-25 NKJV*

Then early 2019, God gave me a message for Apostle W in a dream. The message was that God would forgive him if he genuinely repents and turns back to Him. I didn't totally understand the message, but I unblocked him, delivered the message, and blocked him again.

I had so many attacks: my ears buzzed whenever I prayed; strange things fell off my face like dust and flew out of my ears; the moving object in my head intensified, and my Facebook Ministry was attacked. Sometimes I would go online and preach only to myself, but I persisted and never gave up because I knew that was what the false prophet and the witches wanted: that I should give up on the work of God and quit. But I am not a quitter. Quitters never win. With the help of God, I can do all things. (Philippians 4:13).

> *I can do all things through Christ who strengthens me.*
> *Philippians 4:13 NKJV*

I took two months break off Facebook preaching, but God sent a word to me through His servant, Prophet Shammar, who also preaches on Facebook, to get busy with His business. So, I had to go back preaching. God encourages me, especially when I feel most discouraged; he sends in testimonies. Then, I am reminded of the scripture, that 'many are the afflictions of the righteous, but the Lord delivers him from them all,' and I hold on to it.

Many are the afflictions of the righteous, but the Lord delivers him out of them all.
Psalm 34:19 NKJV

Even my family members are very unsupportive, but I thank God for the strength and encouragement to continue His work. The WOG, Evagelist Princess Belemzy, has also been a great source of encouragement and inspiration. When I see all she does for God and all the hours spent on Facebook doing the work of God, I draw strength and become even more resolute not to give up.

About mid-2019, Apostle W fell sick and was admitted to the hospital for almost a month. This was after I had given the message from God. I don't know if he repented or not. One of his sons sent me a message via WhatsApp, and in my sympathy, I informed the Woman of God so that she could pray for him.

The Woman of God Princess Belemzy is always preaching about forgetting the wrong people have done to us and instead focusing on the good; so that we could forgive them and move on. I decided to visit the Apostle in the hospital. He was in terrible shape, delirious, and unable to recognize me. I sat with his wife for about an hour and told her that he needed deliverance.

He spoke to me in his delirious state, asking if I knew they could pray for the thing on my head to leave. I had never told him of the movements or buzzing I felt in my head; so, I wondered how he knew. I noted this and kept it in mind. On getting home, I cried out to God to forgive and heal him.

Days later, God gave me a dream of Apostle W in white clothing, healed and healthy. So, I went back to the hospital to let him know that God would heal him and he left the hospital some weeks later, fully recovered.

When I got to the hospital, he recognized me but had no recollection of my earlier visit. I met some of his family members and the Ghanaian Pastor friend of his with whom I got into a conversation. He asked why I left the church, and I told him I was in Apostle W's church for ten years and there was no significant difference between the life I lived in the world and the one in that church. Now though, I love God more and no longer live in sin.

Since his family was there, I couldn't bring up the conversation I had with the other lady minister. But Apostle W made a fascinating statement, "Why do you believe in the Woman of God Princess Belemzy and Bishop B but not in me?" At that time, Bishop B had not been exposed by God as a false prophet. But what troubled me was that he wanted me to believe in him and not God. This weighed on my mind. He was directing and wanting people to believe in him and not Jesus Christ, which is a trait of false prophets and teachers I later learned. After this visit to the hospital, I forgave him and unblocked him but didn't have any close contact with him.

In November, a Bishop who had earlier visited the church came around and asked to see me. He was staying at the Apostle's house; so, I went over. We talked and prayed. Then, the Apostle said he wanted to have a conversation with me. I had not seen him since he was discharged from the hospital; so, I decided to listen to him.

His wife and kids were not at home, and when I asked, he told me she had left home after he got back from the hospital. She was tired of all the cheating and infidelity, mostly as the Apostle had made some confessions of the women he had slept with while on the hospital bed, thinking he was dying. He blamed his wife that she never agreed to do what he wanted. Then I asked him, "What about what your wife wants? Is that not important too?"

I started seeing even more how selfish Apostle W was. Everything had to be about him. I made it clear that I only came to see him because the WOG, Princess Belemzy, had convinced me to. He started talking about his marriage again how there has never been love in the marriage, which was why he was cheating. But I knew that was a flagrant lie. Love is not found by sleeping with multiple women at the same time. He admitted that he had an affair with the lady minister at Bethel even when our affair was on. And those were just the ones I was aware of. He also confided in me that he had a relationship with the WOG, one of the ladies from the school, who also joined the church. Mind you, both of these women were married, just as the Apostle.

I asked him about being in a cult, but his response in his own words was, "I will never bow to another God." He begged me to come back to the church, and I wondered what church he was referring to, with all the rot and sin going on there. It sounded more like a strip club to me. I spent all the years in his church supporting him, serving under him, being loyal to him, defending him, and not knowing who he was. I left his house utterly disappointed.

Apostle W did not change, after this conversation, his near-death experience and admission at the hospital; he continued lying. He called the WOG, Princess Belemzy, to thank her for encouraging me to come back and mend the bridge between us. Then he lied to her that he really helped me and even bought me a car, he never bought a car for me, only helped in choosing my car. I do not remember this man even paying for gas in my vehicle. All he knew to do was to take and kept taking. Even if you don't have cash, he would ask to use your credit card, partly why I still have debts on my credit card.

False prophets will drain you, collect whatever they can from you, and then cage you, so you don't prosper. You leave their church worse than you came in and much farther away from God. False prophets never stop lying, scamming or afflicting others unless they repent or when they die. Run away from them and seek deliverance because if you don't, you will still be caged and unable to do successfully the work God has for you.

False prophets love women who are anointed and have a call of God upon their lives. This is so they can steal their anointing and use their star to shine. When I went to Bethel, I didn't even know I had the call of God upon my life, but Apostle W saw it and tried to discourage me every step of the way. Even when it seems they are encouraging you, they have stolen your anointing; you end up not doing much except walking in circles.

When I left the church, Minister Sandra had this dream in which I took all my gifts from the church in a box, and one of the pastors came to beg me to bring back the box. I didn't even know I had all these gifts, but I remember Apostle W asking me to pray for him and for a lady at church who had been having miscarriages. I did not know why then, but now, I understand that he couldn't pray for her because God was not in him. This false prophet, Apostle W has destroyed a lot of destinies, marriages, scammed so many people out of money and still unrepentant. But judgment is here and he has been exposed as the wicked voodoo priest he is masquerading as a servant of God.

Exposure of the False Prophet

I thought I escaped from false prophet Apostle W. even though I still had some doubts not to accuse a servant of God falsely. Unknowingly, I was still watching one false prophet on Facebook, Bishop B., who happened to be the spiritual father of Princess Belemzy.

Early 2020, as I watched his live-streamed church service on Facebook, I dozed off and had a dream. I saw a huge bed in his church, and while he was preaching, there were two ladies on the bed, not paying attention to what he was saying. I thought the dream was from the devil and wondered at the devil's wickedness against this servant of God. I also saw myself resisting Bishop B. in another dream as he was trying to sleep with me. He said he was going to marry me, so it didn't matter if we slept together. I refused and told him it's only after marriage that anything can happen. I blamed the devil for both dreams.

I got a text from Apostle W. reminding me of something he helped me to accomplish. Knowing his manipulative ways, I just responded with 'thanks to God for making everything perfect in His time,' and that ended the conversation.

Then I had a dream around early March 2020. Apostle W. was with three witches and was being whopped by his master for failing his assignment. On waking up, I reminded myself that God doesn't whoop anyone for failing an assignment. Instead, He gives them another chance to get it right. I knew the master in that dream was the devil. So, I quickly blocked his phone and went ahead to block him on Facebook the very next day when God reminded me in a dream.

Please, children of God, pay attention to your dreams. God speaks to His children a lot in dreams and visions. It is true the devil may try to manipulate them, but the ones that God really wants you to see, He makes sure you see them. The dream was not really a shocker. God was only confirming to me that Apostle W. was not His servant. Looking back, I realized there had been so many leadings and warnings which I ignored and overlooked because of the spell over me.

We were on a fast with the WOG Princess Belemzy, and during this fast, God spoke through the mouth of the WOG, vindicating the WOG and informing us that Bishop B had never been His because he worshiped strange gods and his powers were from the marine kingdom. We were all shocked as no one saw this coming. Some people believed it was God speaking through the WOG, while others did not. I believed right away because I had seen God speak through another lady.

What got my attention was the similarity between what God was revealing to us about Bishop B. and his doings and escapades of Apostle W. It was the final confirmation that I needed to believe that Apostle W was not of God but also used strange powers. God said through the WOG Princess Belemzy that judgment would be coming for all these false teachers and prophets, another confirmation of the dream I had in which Apostle W's master was whopping him for not accomplishing his assignment, being judged by his own master.

After listening to what God said, especially the part about sleeping around with women, I unblocked Apostle W. on WhatsApp. I sent him a text telling him what God had said concerning Bishop B., his use of marine powers, and how much it reminded me of him. I told him to repent or face God's judgment. Apostle W. saw the text but never responded to it.

God also said all those afflicted by false prophets should come to the WOG and tell their story and get their deliverance. I was led to text the WOG and tell her all that Apostle W had been doing and that he was also a false prophet, and I was also a victim of a false prophet. I had a dream with a voice telling me to go, go. I knew this was God telling me to speak publicly about the false prophet, Apostle W., so others could be set free. I had spoken about him on the WOG's Facebook platform, but God also wanted me to tell my story on my page, and the WOG prophesied this.

The WOG Belema prayed for me, and I got my deliverance. So, I took to my platform to share my story.

My name on Facebook is Min Felicia Tengu, and my Fan Page on Facebook is Jesus Loves You UnConditionally.

After this exposure, the persecution was great. People put up Facebook status just to insult and abuse me. I didn't care because God led me, and I know that what I did pleased God. God even gave me a Word through His prophet, Shammar Bennet, that my testimony would bring many people to the foot of the cross, and God also gave me a ministry to help hurting women.

My Mess has become my Message and created a Ministry for me. This is Prophet Shammar's prophecy to me in his words: *Minister Felicia, Minister Felicia, the Lord speaks to me. The Lord told me to tell you this: that your Testimonies are going to increase Your Testimonies are going to draw people at the foot of the cross, so said the Lord.*

I have gotten numerous testimonies following my obedience to God to tell my story. Indeed, some people right now are not happy with me; they are insulting and persecuting me, but what matters is that my Heavenly Father is pleased by my obedience and exposure of this false prophet, Apostle W. Obeying God is what matters in life: pleasing God, and doing His will, and not being a man-pleaser.

Now, I completely understand God's Word, which talks about God turning around the evil meant for one to good. Remember the story of Joseph:

But as for you, you meant evil against me; but God meant it for good, in order to bring it about as it is this day, to save many people alive.

Genesis 50:20 NKJV

What the devil and the false prophet intended to use to harm and disgrace me, God is turning it around for my good.

And we know that all things work together for good to those who love God, to those who are the called according to His purpose.
Romans 8:28 NKJV

A particular lady, who along with her husband, attended Bethel, reached out to me and told me of a day the Apostle tried to kiss her forcefully, but she resisted. She reported the incident to her husband but the husband, being a leader at Bethel, did nothing. Instead, he asked her what she wanted him to do asides from harassing the Apostle.

Apparently, the husband is also under a spell. The lady left the church not too long after that incident but had lost her peace since then. She faced problems in her marriage and could not sleep well for almost six years because of fear. Nothing was working in her life, and she kept battling stagnation and limitation.

I prayed for her, and she was able to get some peace and sleep after so many years. She also finally got a job after a long time. Glory to God almighty. According to her, it was as if a burden had been lifted off her shoulders. She wrote a testimony of what happened, and I posted it on Facebook. However, this particular testimony disappeared from my page, telling me that this false prophet (Voodoo priests as God calls them) is monitoring my page and must have reported the testimony as inappropriate.

As I earlier said, false prophets will drain you. In the name of giving God 'Painful Sacrifices', a friend was scammed of her life savings ($50,000) by Bishop B. the false prophet. False prophets will take everything from you, even your life.

As time went on at Princess Belemzy Ministries, many people have come forward to tell their stories of being victims of false prophets. Many have received their deliverance and breakthroughs. God is teaching us a lot about false prophets, and I have come to realize that there are many more false prophets and teachers than I ever imagined.

If you are in the church of a false prophet, know that most of the visiting pastors to that church will be fake pastors and false prophets. Their effect is not limited to only you as your family members can be affected through you.

I am beginning to know a lot concerning how false prophets operate. They give prophecies that never come to pass. Even when they tell you something evil the devil is planning against you, they cannot pray to cancel it. Instead, they make those evil prophecies come to pass in your life.

Do not allow just anyone prophesy over your life. They might just be declaring evil and doom over you. God reminded me of a private prophetic word that the false prophet, Apostle W., gave to a lady at church. He told her not to go out on a particular weekend, but this lady went out, had an accident, and sustained injuries she never recovered from. God reminding me of that incident indicates that Apostle W knew what happened to that lady.

Another incident comes to mind. Apostle W prophesied to a lady at the church that something evil would happen to her mum. He advised she should come to the church for seven days to pray and cancel whatever evil was meant. This lady never went for the private prayer sessions, and I believe it was because she didn't trust him, and she was also married. Truly, not too long after the prophecy, the lady's mother suffered a heart attack during service at her church and died.

False prophets are wicked. They will afflict and even kill you and your family. Run away from them and expose them!

After I told my story on Facebook, the moving objects in my head intensified. But I keep getting my deliverance as I pray and also watch the WOG. These voodoo priests never stop sending afflictions, but God keeps delivering me.

God calls Princess Belemzy Ministries 'The School of Power', and God has taught us a lot about false prophets. Many of God's children have been suffering because of a lack of knowledge concerning false prophets and teachers.

My people are destroyed for lack of knowledge.
Because you have rejected knowledge,
I also will reject you from being priest for Me; Because you have forgotten the law of your God, I also will forget your children.
Hosea 4:6 NKJV

I learned about some of the charms these false prophets wear, chains with mermaids on them, and rings with which they cast spells on unsuspecting believers. I thought most of these things were part of the dressing for men of God, but now I know better. Apostle W. also had some of these rings and chains.

It has been confirmed that the Pastor I spent ten years of my life submitted to, serving God with my whole heart, supporting him, and defending, is a false prophet. This false prophet, Apostle W. has destroyed a lot of destinies, marriages, scammed so many people out of money and is still unrepentant and with no remorse. But judgment is here and he has been exposed as the wicked voodoo priest he is, masquerading as a servant of God.

After my exposure of Apostle W. on Facebook, it was brought to my attention that he slept with a lot of other women at the church, this false prophet is so evil, slept with mother and daughter with no remorse, slept with sisters, even in one family slept with mother, daughter and sister to the mother, and I am still rattled hearing all this. A couple from the church also visited me and reported Apostle W. and one of his family members also scammed them of about $10,000 in a bid to help them be regular in the US. It is a huge disappointment, but I don't regret it because I can tell my story and help other women and men who are also victims of false prophets through my experience. Together, we can recognize and expose them.

In everything give thanks; for this is the will of God in Christ Jesus for you.

1 Thessalonians 5:18 *NKJV*

The word of God says we should give Him thanks in all situations, so I give God thanks for all that happened to me for I know there is a reason why it happened.

False Prophets are Scammers and Voodoo Priests behind the Pulpit

False Prophets are Scammers and Voodoo Priests behind the Pulpit. Instead of staying in their shrines, these men/women use God's house and name to hide their Voodoo practices. False prophets are very evil, and there are a lot of them all over the world. Only Jesus can deliver us from them.

God wants us to expose the works of the devil. These false prophets and false teachers have been afflicting God's children for so long, and He is furious. God spoke through my mother in the Lord, Evangelist Princess Belemzy, that He has passed Judgment on all the false prophets and teachers who do not want to repent.

Some of them are already demonized and unable to repent and will face their Judgment. God gave her the MANDATE, POWER, AND ANOINTING to expose false prophets worldwide and DELIVER their VICTIMS who come to her for DELIVERANCE.

You can find her on Facebook at Princess Belemzy Ministries, Belema Abili, on YouTube, Twitter, and Instagram.

The false prophets and teachers have turned God's church into a voodoo house and platform to scam and afflict people. God has heard the cries of His children and wants these false prophets and teachers exposed.

God loves all His children and wants us to have abundant life on this earth, fulfill our destinies, and make heaven; not to be slaves to false prophets or teachers and suffer afflictions and miss heaven in the end.

False prophets love no one but themselves; they might fool you to think they love you, but deep down, they hate you, and if they get the chance, may even kill you for the constant rituals and sacrifices to their gods. Some of them rape women to fulfill these rituals and also as a form of worship to their gods.

False prophets and teachers never wish anybody any good. They are ready and willing to take anything they can get from you and pay you back with afflictions. They DO NOT know God and have no relationship with Him. They pray to the devil and worship the devil because they are his servants.

False prophets and teachers are very manipulative and will fool you into thinking otherwise concerning them. With their spells and charms, they can get you to love them and do whatever they want you to do for them.

On reading this book, if you realize that the servant of God you are submitted to is a false prophet or teacher, you have to do the right thing by leaving. Don't stay with them or cover up for them. They have caused you great harm, and while you might not see it physically, the damage in the spiritual realm is real and significant. God asks us in His Word to have no fellowship with the evil works of the devil but to expose them.

And have no fellowship with the unfruitful works of darkness, but rather expose them.

Ephesians 5:11 NKJV

God expects us as His children to expose the works of the false prophets and teachers because they are from the pit of hell. They cage you such that you cannot progress in life and everything concerning you is stagnant; physically, spiritually, financially, etc.

They get your money and lock it up, so you don't prosper, and even when they give you money, it is to drain the finances you have. False prophets and teachers steal your glory and whatever gifting and anointing God has given you to shine and prosper.

If they have slept with you, they have deposited a lot of evil in you, which need to be cast out of you by deliverance. They marry you spiritually, and you are not able to marry physically. Even if you succeed in getting married, the marriage will not last. This is because, spiritually, they are your spouse and are having sex with you at all times, and you belong to them. For women, they will promise you marriage, which most likely won't happen, and keep sleeping with you before the marriage with deceitful assurances that God already recognizes the marriage spiritually. Do not believe this lie from the pit of hell. These evil ones may even get you pregnant and coerce, convince or threaten you to terminate the pregnancy so they can use it for their evil rituals.

They tie up your destiny, and you cannot walk in the purpose God created you for, nor fulfill your destiny. God has good plans for all His children and wants us to fulfill those plans here on earth. In His word (Jeremiah 29:11), He wants a good life for us all, not to be slaves to false prophets, being manipulated, used, and afflicted by them.

For I know the thoughts that I think toward you, says the Lord, thoughts of peace and not of evil, to give you a future and a hope.
Jeremiah 29:11 NKJV

One of the afflictions of false prophets and teachers comes in the form of moving objects. These are strange movements in your body that you cannot identify their cause. They are spiritual snakes sent to you, especially to your head, which come with significant discomfort and can sometimes make you feel crazy.

Beware of false prophets and teachers. Before asking anyone for prayers and submitting yourself to any church, pray to God about it and check out (test) if the Spirit is from God. Trust no one except God. My experience was a very unpleasant one, and I don't wish it on anyone, but I learned a lot through this experience.

I thank God for protecting and keeping me and not letting the false prophets or witches kill me. Despite all my sins before knowing God and all I did with the false prophet, I turned to God, cried out for mercy and forgiveness, and He forgave me, anointed me, and is now using me for His glory. They set a trap for me, but Jesus delivered me, and now I am as free as a bird. (Psalm 124:7). The VINDICATION of the WOG Princess Belemzy has vindicated us all from the trap of false prophets and teachers.

> *Our soul has escaped as a bird from the snare of the fowlers;*
> *The snare is broken, and we have escaped.*
> *Psalm 124:7 NKJV*

If you need someone to confide in, pray with, or for Godly counsel, you can contact me on Facebook, Min Felicia Tengu. My Fan Page is Jesus Loves You Unconditionally, and on YouTube, Jesus Loves You Unconditionally Ministries.

God is ready to forgive you no matter what you have done or the pit you currently find yourself in. We have a merciful and loving Father who does not want any of us to perish or be won over by the devil. If you are ready to repent and turn to God, place your right hand across your heart and say this salvation prayer from your heart:

Prayer

Dear Lord,

I confess I am a sinner. Please forgive my sins for I didn't know any better, I promise not to go back to my old ways

Father, I believe you sent your Son Jesus Christ who came and died on the cross of Calvary

And rose three days later to save me from my sins and give me eternal life.

I receive Jesus Christ into my heart and life to be my Lord and personal Savior and Lord over my life.

I ask all these in Jesus' name. Amen. Say I am a child of God. I love you, Jesus.

Be filled with the Holy Spirit, and may it be made manifest in you through speaking in tongues, if you so desire.

Read your Bible. Begin with the Gospel as recorded by Matthew, Mark, Luke, and John. Pray always and about everything. Run away from false prophets and teachers; they will only lead you to hell.

Be blessed.

REMEMBER JESUS LOVES YOU UNCONDITIONALLY!

ALL THE GLORY BELONGS TO GOD.